Drowning in D
(Corporate

Forward:

The purpose of this book is to help CEO's, CIO's, and CTO's or Managers make decisions based on numbers and not just the recommendations of the people under them. We give real life examples, and useful questions to ask your personnel. We give you true stories, along with lessons learned. You don't have to learn from the school of hard knocks at your company.

> As an administrator, you don't need to know the details, but it's good to understand when these strategies are discussed what people are asking to build.

In this book, the word "Migration" will be used almost exclusively for Conversions, Migrations, ETL, Integrations, etc. The reason for this is simple. "Migrations" implies repeatability, and in my experience, data is never moved just once without issues. If the process is designed for repeatability, IMHO, you get a better "one-time" move too.

Because some migrations involve multi-disciplinary teams, the topic of dealing with people will be one focus of this book. It is not my intent to tell you how to deal with your people, but to point out possible issues and possible ways to deal with them.

Acknowledgements:

Jerry would like to thank his wife, and his kids, for putting up with the time this book required him to spend away from them. He would also like to thank CEOSpace for giving him the idea for the book and the resources to make it a reality.

About the authors of this book:
Jerry Hayward

Jerry has been performing data conversions since 1995, and has performed conversions over the years for companies he was employed by. He also did conversions for his employers' clients as part of his job, and these companies include ACS, KLA Tencor, and NASA, just to name a few.

Jerry's conversions have moved data for ACS (General business Workflow processes), several BlueCross BlueShield organizations (healthcare industry), TEM companies (Telecom), and everything in between. Jerry has worked with Systems that spanned the globe, data warehouses measured in Petabytes, and systems so small that the imports and exports were in MS Excel™ spreadsheets.

Over the years Jerry has been on teams, on his own, authored tools, written "One-off Code", used tools supplied by third parties, and taken over conversions started by others. Jerry has been on successful conversions and conversion failures which were not allowed to die. This book is his attempt to help others avoid making mistakes and benefit from his sometimes unfortunate experiences.

Jerry is also the author of the *Drowning in Data: Personal edition.*

Jerry founded the company Convertabase Inc. (http://www.convertabase.com) which has an educational section to teach data conversion, as well as offering free and fee tools for use.

Sam Shumway

Sam Shumway has been involved with many computer companies over his 30+ years of computer experience. He has worked for both small and large companies, such as Gazelle Systems, Texas Instruments, and Symantec.

Sam has worked on teams involved in data backup, security software, data compression, and data publishing dealing with issues involving data design, presentation, and data usability. In the past he has done conversions for telecom from six Wireless vendors to a SQL server database, MySQL and others. He helped design and build an innovative EDI-to-SQL single-pass converter, as well as numerous data automation solutions.

Sam is also co-author of the *Drowning in Data: Personal edition.*

Sam is the CTO of Convertabase Inc. (http://www.convertabase.com) which has an educational section to teach data conversion, as well as offers some free and some fee tools on it.

Index

7. Verifying a data migration.

8. Executing a data migration.

9. Documenting your data migration.

10. Planning for the future.

11. Business process system

12. Workflow process system

The 22 undeniable truths of data migration

1. It's not simple.
2. No quote is "Firm".
3. Scalability is a myth.
4. There isn't enough room.
5. There are always exceptions.
6. It needs to be "done yesterday".
7. Data migration is not glamorous.
8. There is never enough documentation.
9. The person you need to talk to is "Out".
10. It will always take longer than you thought.
11. You can't modify the schema to make it work.
12. The process only blows up when not monitored.
13. Specifications are not complete until the project is.
14. 80% of your effort will be spent on 20% of your data.
15. You don't have access rights to the data you need most.
16. Data is never as clean, or as organized as you were told it is.
17. No one will know who the developer is, unless he messes up.
18. Over time, one-off code will always be more expensive than tools.
19. The person who ends up migrating the data is the least experienced.
20. Only when the project is completed will you know what was forgotten.
21. The importance of data is directly proportional to how hard it is to access.

22. A person assigned to a migration project will try to be assigned to anything else.

Corollaries:
1. Inexperienced programmers tend to take a bottom up approach. "I'll start coding, and this will all make sense." This leads to dead ends, and wasted time.
2. Experienced programmers tend to take a top down approach. Define the problem in enough detail, and the most efficient method will readily become apparent.
3. The "that-won't-be-a-big-issue" problems are the hardest to solve.
4. The backed-up code from the "last time we did this" is missing the most essential pieces.

Self-serve Vs Pay at the pump

Perspectives are tricky things; they cannot be given, only acquired.

Many years ago, gas stations had a bunch of young men who would run out to your car, check your tires, and engine oil, and wash your windshield. In general, they made you feel like a king. "Full Service" was the motto.

One day, in the name of profit, all those eager young men disappeared, and Self-Serve became the norm. The theory was that customers would put up with the lack of service in order to get cheaper prices; but of course, the gas stations were making more money too. The Customers pumped their gas in rain, snow, or shine; then went to wait in line while a surly cashier who never moved from behind bullet-proof glass took their money through a slot. The customers were not happy, but they needed gasoline, and all the service stations seemed be doing the same thing. If you wanted gas, you bought at the local station since they were the only providers around.

One day, also in the name of profit, gas companies started putting ATM and credit card machines right in the pump. "Pay-at-the-Pump" was born, with no more surly Cashiers, and no more grumpy, wet customers. People loved Pay-at-the-Pump, unlike Self-Serve.

Both services made the company more profitable, but Pay-at-the-Pump was perceived as being a real convenience for the customer. It was a convenience, but it also meant that service stations didn't keep as many cashiers on staff and saved money.

Most IT departments have a "Self-Serve" attitude, when their attitude should be a "Pay-at-the-Pump" one. Pay-at-the-Pump makes more money than Self-Serve when people have a choice; after all, when it's raining, you're almost out of gas, and there are two identically-priced stations side by side, but only one of them has Pay-at-the-Pump, you probably won't patronize the one with only Self-Serve and a required cashier?

It's raining now.

Even if your customers don't directly interface with your business's database (like buying stuff and placing orders on the web), they can only do what your employees let them do; so if an employee can't do it, neither can the customer. Most customers will relish the idea of being able to buy when it's convenient for them. Buying things on the web is a convenience that's a "Pay-at-the-Pump" mentality. If a migration can get you to that level of perceived service, you should add it to your ROI calculation—but we'll get to that.

In today's Global economy, odds are your customers can get what you sell them, or a product close to it somewhere else. If they can't—wait a bit. Soon they will be able to. Your company is dependent on your customers having a good internet experience; because on the internet, all gas stations are theoretically right next to each other.

In this book, we will focus on "Pay-at-the-Pump" Solutions.

How to tell when your company needs a data migration.

If you don't know what you don't know, then you can't tell what you need to learn...

Examine your current system

Analyzing your company's data can take lots of time and effort, so how do you know when to do the analysis without slowing your business?

Knowing when to move data can keep a company in control of its market, its competitors, and will ultimately improve its bottom line.

First, analyze your business for "Down Time". If you have a seasonal business, plan to do your Maintenance in the off-season. If your business is not seasonal, and you need to find out when your down-times are, ask your DBA, or whoever builds reports, to show a report of some quantitative way, such as orders, new members, or record creation, to measure when you are busy making money. Tell this report builder that you want to see when the system is least-used by time of day, and day of month, and monthly. (This is a useful report even if you don't need to move data) Many companies cannot come up with all of this data, but you should be able to get something. This report will tell you when to perform maintenance on your system, and when to plan a migration should you determine the company needs one. (If you have no downtime, is your system really set up for that? If not, migrate to one that is.)

There are some free tools on http://www.convertabase.com that will help you analyze your database, if you don't have tools already.

Next, ask your employees (sales, fulfillment, secretaries, etc.) the following questions:

- What do you spend the most time doing?

- What annoys you the most about our system?

- What costs the company the most due to our system?

- Are there things you'd like to know, but can't figure out?

- Are there things that can only be done manually? If so, what?

- Are there things about our system that make our customers unhappy?

- Are customers always telling you, "We updated the address during the last call!"?

- Does the company enter the same information into more than one system? If yes; what is being entered more than once?

- Do we have information on systems that are obsolete? (3-5 years old is obsolete.)

- Add any other open-ended questions that are appropriate for your industry when you do this information-gathering process.

Find out how much time is being spent on unnecessary tasks. How much are you paying Employees to do unnecessary tasks?

If you don't have a formula for the cost of inefficiency, start with this:

(Hourly Salary + benefits) * 1.2 = Hourly Cost of Inefficiency. (1.2 is for HR, etc.)

Then, take the Hourly Cost of Inefficiency, and multiply that by the Hours lost. Then multiply again by the number of people in that position. Finally, add the costs for all the positions with inefficiencies.

Many companies have a culture that scares people and discourages them from listing places where they are inefficient. In this case, you might want to make the survey anonymous, or multiply your result by a modifier to get your final number; this modifier will vary based on corporate culture.

In one company I analyzed, they had an old machine that they were afraid to turn off. There was only one person who was allowed to enter data in that machine; so they would print out their entry screen for the main system, and pile the printouts up on her in-box. Then, she would periodically run down the hall, up a flight of stairs, over to the machine, and re-enter all the data. They were embarrassed to admit what they were doing on a questionnaire, but in a personal conversation, we got that "little" gem of information. She reported that it really didn't bother her until she was 5 months pregnant. When I spoke to her, she was in her eighth month. The risk of failure and loss of data in the next three years was estimated at 100%

> When the risk is 100%, that justifies a migration all by itself.

What is the risk to a business with a process like this? A dependency on one person running down a hall, up the stairs, and manually entering data on a machine so old no one is willing to turn it off for fear it will never turn on again? I submit that this company's ROI could be huge for getting their system migrated to a modern system.

Research the options

If you don't know what all your options are, how can you be sure you are picking the right one?

Now, you need to decide, when you have a problem, if you should fix your existing system or replace it.

> Don't do your survey until you have read the whole book! We will add to what should be in the survey throughout the book.

Continue by asking your employees questions again.

Ask your employees what they think the solution should be. (You can add this to your first survey and do both at once…but it may overwhelm them.) Ask them how they currently solve the problems they are reporting. Some of them may have better solutions than others, such as a spreadsheet they have created or an application they use. Deploy that application first for immediate efficiency increases! Often, a small piece of middleware can yield a huge return.

Here are some questions to ask your IT people:

- Can the current system be fixed? (Just fix what the users say is broken, please…)

- How much would their proposed solution cost? (Ask them to look at In-house work, hiring Consultants, and purchased software solutions, and then give you a price for each.)

- How much does it cost to maintain the current system? (Ask "What are your cost projections for the next three years?")

- Can I plan for future growth? (Ask "Can I get a report on past growth from the system?" and "What are the growth projections for our current system for the next three years?" and "What is our system's capacity?") While an IT department could fudge these numbers, in my experience they won't. The odds of getting caught are high, so they will do their best on these projections.

> **IT Departments do not, as a rule, turn down the chance to spend money.**

I would **not** ask the IT department **if** you need a new system, because I have never seen an IT department say NO to an upgrade opportunity. Ask for their assessment first, and then decide if you see enough ROI to justify the investment (making the money back in two-to-five years.) Then, with the numbers in front of them, ask the IT department what they recommend.

> **Ask the IT to justify the numbers.**

Sometimes there is not one "perfect" solution. You may have to buy part, and build part. Ask the IT department to justify the numbers. Tell them you will be hiring a consultant to go over the justification. You will never lose by having two qualified sets of eyes on the "plan." Also, ask the IT department to identify "Low Hanging Fruit" in the form of cheap ways to take advantage of a migration's result to add value or functionality for their users (the people who will actually use the system.)

If they recommend a whole new system, ask them to prepare the ROI worksheet found in this book, and always remind them they will have to justify the numbers.

In order to decide if you are going to do this at all, you need to know what each of your variables are: Who is going to do the migration, how they will do it, and how much that will cost.

Think about these choices before you begin:

- **Making the software vendor do the migration.** Most venders of software, especially databases, have some kind of migration service they offer. Ask them:

  - o Have they converted to/from your other software before?

  - o What tools will they use?

  - o Did they build or buy those tools?

- Are they hiring a consultant and handing the migration off to them?

- If they don't hire consultants themselves or offer migration tools, do they have a company they recommend for the job?

- If they have no recommendation, is there a commercial migration package specifically designed for what you are doing? To find out, ask your vendor(s), search the web, and ask other people you know who are running the same software…)

- When you find migration software, you need to know who can run it. Does it require a DBA, Programmer, or Business Analyst?

- How much does it cost?

- How is the cost calculated? (Server License Agreement, User/Seat license, Both Licenses, Number of records, Time Involved?)

- Can you talk to real people who have used the migration software you're considering?

- **Hiring your own Consulting company(s).** If possible, ask another corporation that hired them these questions:

  o Have they worked with either piece of software?

  o How much did it cost the company that hired them?

  o How long did it take?

  o Is the lead person available?

  o Do they give free estimates?

  o Who owns the code when they get done?

  o How much documentation will you get on the process?

  o How much input can you have on the migration?

- **Doing it Yourself.** If you do it yourself, ask IT:

  o Do they have the personnel?

  o Does their personal have the skills?

  o Do they have the time?

- o What will Training cost?

- o What if my people leave before the project is complete?

- o What if my people need help?

- o How much does support cost?

- o As you gather this information, ask what the risk of failure is, and what it would cost to fix such a failure. Add that risk to the cost in the ROI calculation.

If you find out that the vendor will be hiring a consultant who has not done this before, get your own consultant! Do it yourself! At least, then, you will actually know what is going on.

Calculate the return

If you don't know what you are buying, don't spend the money.

If you have a "Mandate" from your board, or a legal requirement, the ROI may not matter. You may just have to "do it." I still like to perform this step so I know what I am doing to my budget (If you have been told to just do it, and the ROI isn't there, it's a good time to ask for an increased budget. Without this step, you just don't know.)

> Calculate ROI before starting every project, even if it's mandated.

Data migrations can make or break a company. The long conversion process can be a drain on resources and staff. The only time you want to take that "hit" is when it will be worth it. ROI, or Return on Investment, sounds simple, but what factors make up the return, and what make up the investment?

> Don't fudge the numbers on an assessment. Assessments are tools, not traps, if you don't like the result; either don't tell anyone, or find a legitimate reason to change the input

In your research, you should have gained an idea what

the investment would be. Once you have prices for multiple ways to do this migration, add risk factors and down-time costs to the methods available. Then pick the one you are most comfortable with. Once you know what you are going to do, if you do anything, start compiling a table of Investments and Returns. You can fudge this table. If you want to fudge your result, that's easy: Only fill in one side, and poof, it's profitable (or not) as you wish.

Some Suggestions to consider for your list:

Investment	Return
Software costs (Are you paying a license fee now?	Software savings (Will there be a license fee for this?)
Manpower cost: (consultants, additional employees needed for the migration)	Manpower savings (eliminated positions for 3 to five years)
Support fees for the old system (these always go up when a system is obsolete)	Support fees for the new system (lock in as low of a rate as you can for as long as you can)
Features needed by your company that you would have to build	Features needed by your company that you no longer have to build

Old Hardware support cost	Hardware you can phase out.
Opportunity cost (Risk multiplied by the likelihood of it happening)	New opportunities (Opportunities, like web access, Increased business opportunities?)

These are just a few examples. Be thorough, but don't get ridiculous.

Once you have all the things that matter in your table, assign dollar values to them. Don't forget that this is over time, so you may want to build a spread sheet and calculate for several years at once. Sometimes a migration that makes no sense for a three year ROI is wonderful at four years when your current contract expires and you go for a new support contract. It may also change when your projections for your costs spike, etc. Now, add up all the investments and returns, divide the return by the investment, and you should get a multiple like 3.25, or 4.5. If the return does not meet your corporate standards, then don't do it. Sit pat and keep doing what you are doing. If you still think you should do it, try thinking of more things your migration will impact.

Do not cheat on your numbers. Don't try to get cheaper quotes to make the ROI "work out." Anything worth doing is worth doing well.

If you are looking at an expensive in-house figure, consider buying or licensing tools for a short period of time to get your employees a cheaper way of doing things. Convertabase offers its tools on line at www.convertabase.com.

Sometimes, it's tempting to pick someone you know because of your relationship which can be the most expensive choice (**Recuse yourself** if family is involved).

There was a large multinational fast food company that had an ERP (Enterprise Resource Planning) system which they had refused to upgrade for years because the customizations they had done to the old system would have to be done all over again to the new system. This system ran their just-in-time deliveries worldwide.

A new version of their ERP software was released by the vendor which finally pushed their old version into the sunset provisions of the vendor's contract. They could not buy support for the old system at any price; suddenly the ROI was there for them, and in spades (See my section on planning for the future).

They asked the vendor how to get their data from where it was on the old system to the new system. They were told, "Buy every interim upgrade, and run them back-to-back.

You should be done in six months—tops."
Obviously, this was unacceptable for them.

I was called in, and ran my tools (see
www.convertabase.com to get a look at my
tools) to get an idea of the problem. I quoted
them a cost of $250,000 and time-frame of
four months to skip over two whole major
revisions of their software and move their data
to the most recent version. They asked for a
formal proposal, which I produced and sent
them the next day. (Automated documentation
is so cool…)

I never heard back from them, and they
stopped taking my calls. I wondered what I
had done wrong. Finally, I contacted a friend
who was doing long-term contract work for
them. He told me the VP in charge had
received an identical proposal from a
competing consulting firm the day after mine
had been delivered. The only thing different
was the cover sheet! (Not suspicious at all…)

Nepotism is not the way to pick vendors.

It turned out that the VP's son worked at the
"Competitor." The company decided to go
with the competitor, since there was no
difference in the quote. I could have made a
fuss about having my work plagiarized, but I
knew I could not win the day, so I decided to

watch and see what would happen when this "Competitor" tried to do with "one-off code. I knew my tools could do the job in two months (Which included testing after the migration was up and running).

I kept checking in with my friend about how things were going there. Finally, after two years, and two-and-a-half million dollars later, they did an irreversible Friday-night conversion with the attendant Monday-morning regret. (One-way conversions are non-repeatable, and since you can't test like you do with a migration, are not a good choice, but I digress. Their $2,500,000 cost vs. my $250.000 cost is also not a good choice, but again, I digress.)

The VP made a decision based on a family relationship that really hurt his company, and the whole time people were asking, "What if we'd gone with the other guy?" He'd reply, "We'd have had the same problems with the other guy." While it protected him somewhat, it just wasn't true. Fortunately this company was big enough to absorb the losses.

The moral of this story is no matter how tempting, don't decide based on who you know. Ask for demonstrations of what they can do, and go with demonstrated capability over the "old boy network" every time.

In summary:

- Find your "down time" (Use Reports and Tools)

- Ask your employees about your system. (An employee survey)

- Evaluate how well your system matches your business. (What does it do that you don't need, what does it not do that you do need?)

- Look for ways to measure your system that use empirical data. (Hard numbers are more accurate then feelings).

- Is the current system costing me enough to make a migration worthwhile? (Do the math, even if you think you have to migrate no matter how the math comes out.)

- Find out how much it will cost to do what you think needs to be done.

Overcoming resistance

Resistance can happen for good and bad reasons; the key is to know which you are facing without having to dig too deeply

In many companies any kind of change is met with resistance, and this resistance can come from many sources:

- Simple inertia.

- Empires within the company

- Job security

- Laziness

- Incompetence

- None of the above

No one wants to think their employees, management, or other departments are "plotting against them", but the sad truth is that in some companies politics is more important than the bottom line. I have seen too many companies tangled up in politics to the point that migrations that should save the company money just can't happen. Let's look through the stereotypes of these one at a time:

Simple inertia:

Simple inertia is the easiest to overcome, because it is the easiest to identify. Simple inertia is characterized by the "If it isn't broke don't fix it" mantra. People who ask why the current system is not good enough with the ROI staring them in the face are not being stupid, they just don't want to change. The change in perspective can be as simple as showing them the results of your survey (properly sanitized of course), or a company meeting where the pain of the users (their customers) is aired. When the proposed solution is discussed and can alleviate the pain, or incentives for a quick project can be given, it might win stubborn people over. Sometimes just a one-on-one lunch with the most obvious "no-change-needed person," to discuss what you have uncovered, will be enough.

Empires:

Empires are characterized by lines of authority that are bent or broken inside a company. If you have shipping reporting to IT for example, you may have an empire on your hands. Often these lines of authority are "unofficial", caused by nepotism or a personal obligation, debt, or friendship that is not in the company's best interests.

Empires can be the most difficult to root out because, as a political entity, they are often highly suspicious, and any action can be perceived as a threat to their existence.

I worked for a company where the director of IT was reporting directly to a VP, which is not that unusual, except on the org. chart it was not supposed to be that way.

The director's father had invested in the company on the condition that the VP, a friend of his, would take on his son as an employee of the company.

The company at large knew nothing of this arrangement; neither did the son who was hired.

The VP had planted his own definitions of "Team Player" in this young director's mind. These definitions of "Team Player" were not in the company's best interest.

I was hired into the company at the suggestion of the CEO, who I had worked for previously, and noticed that whenever the VP was stymied in a meeting by someone from another department, that person would start having trouble accessing the corporate software.

The manager over shipping came to me one day after a heated debate with the VP the day before left him unable to run the shipping reports which he needed for a meeting with all the VP's. He asked me to look into it when the director was at lunch. So I looked in the database, and he had been dropped from the group that had access to some of the shipping tables. I reinstated his access, had him log in at my desk, and let him run his reports.

Soon, whenever the IT director was "out," people would come to me to be reinstated. (Not a good sign for me.) Soon, my boss, this director, told me that my job was in question. It got interesting because the VP, not my boss, talked to me about what was going on. He gave me his definition of being a "team player," and I'll do my best to recreate his definition here:

"To be a team player you have to do whatever it takes to make your boss look good, even if it seems wrong at the time.

"Your job is far more than just doing what is on your job description; you need to make your boss look good so he can get raises and promotions.

"As he rises in the company, so do you; when he falls, you may be unemployed as well.

"Your boss protects you, without him you would be fired.

"When your boss looks good, he can make his boss look good, and when his boss looks good, he can make his boss look good, all the way up to the top of the company.

"When the president of the company looks good, the company will do well and your stock will be worth more. "Everybody wins."

I asked, "So how do I know if my boss is making his boss look good with what I do?"

He said "You don't have to worry about that. Just worry about the team you are on, and doing whatever it takes to make your boss look good.

"You see, when your boss says that someone doesn't know how to use the system and that's why they can't access it, and you "fix the system" so they can use it, your boss doesn't look good. So…are you going to be a team player?"

I had always been a "Team Player," but my team was the company. I knew why the CEO had asked them to hire me—he knew he had a problem, just not where it was. He knew I would never play ball with people who were hurting his company.

I knew my days at that job were numbered, so I made sure the whole empire was exposed when that VP had the Director over me fire me while the CEO was on vacation.

The CEO, when he returned, knew what I had done for his company and offered me my former boss's job when I came in for my last check. I had already accepted a position at another company, however.

Empires can kill a company's productivity. Consider how much time was wasted because people could not use the system to do their jobs. How much did that cost the company in revenue, in lost opportunities, and in hiring and training costs as people became frustrated and quit? Consider how an empire adds to the ROI calculation of an investor in the company.

Here are some simple steps to eliminating Empires:

- Cross training. (Every manager should know minimally how to do every other manager's job. Tell them "If you are irreplaceable, you are un-promotable". Empires can only survive in secrecy, so cross training eliminates the mystery of what the other guy does. (Cross training also makes for more relaxing vacations for managers.)

- More than one DBA (If only one guy holds the power of your data, he controls the company. Absolute power corrupts absolutely.)

- IT should answer directly to the CEO or to a committee. (IT is so powerful in today's companies that having them report to any individual person is to give that person the makings of an empire)

- You should ask your employees regularly if they have any obligation to any other employee in the company ($20 is okay, but $100,000 becomes, "Houston! We have a problem!")

- All in-house software should have **clear** error messages for things like locked tables and insufficient access.

Job security:

When the person in question is invaluable now, but will be unemployed or managing fewer people after the migration, you can expect resistance. For example:

> We had a company that was performing a process which took an analyst at least 20 hours to perform—per customer! They had sixteen analysts employed full time. We brought in a tool that would reduce this manual process to 20 minutes. For reasons that escape me, the analysts whose jobs would be lost were assigned to evaluate the tool. They went to fantastic lengths to claim the tool didn't work, even when every demo on their systems, with them

> Analysts can do math; they knew if the company bought the tool, it would only need two or three analysts to do the job.

> running the keyboards, went flawlessly. In the end, the CEO fired all of them, moved processing to another state so the branch there would use the tool, requiring fewer analysts.

Never let the person who is going to be replaced evaluate the software that is going to make them obsolete. Never!

Laziness:

This one's a toughie. Not many employees want to be classed as lazy, especially if they want to keep a job. However, a data Migration is a lot of work, and they may think they're too busy, or are too busy looking busy. Respect your employees' current schedule by asking them for a list of the projects they are on and how much of their day they spend on that. Then have their boss confirm that it's reasonable. Sometimes an employee really is too busy to take the time to sharpen their saw and improve productivity; sometimes the saw is dull from disuse because the employee only uses it when you are around.

Simple solutions when you suspect laziness:

- Offer money or some other inducement, like a company laptop. (Lazy people will often stir themselves for money. If it's apparent they could have done it, but said no because of laziness, consider that in your next review.)

- Offer to get a consultant to help them with their normal tasks during the conversion. A smart (not lazy) employee will take you up on that and work the poor unsuspecting consultant to a frazzle. (Interview the consultant after two weeks to see how hard the guy really is working.)

- Review your performance bonuses, structure them so laziness is not rewarded and go-getter attitudes are. (The lazy people will leave for jobs that reward them because of other people's hard work.)

Once you know what kind of resistance you are going to encounter, you can counter it in your plan for the conversion. Try to finesse resistance if at all possible. A migration is not a good time for a head-to-head argument, even though it happens during migrations. Understand the resistance when you meet it, and finesse it with some of the suggestions here, or something from your own experience.

Incompetence:

This always affects the bottom line in any project. If the employee is willing to admit his inability, you can move forward with training or reassignment. The danger is the employee who strives to hide his incompetence. Often blame, excuses, empires, misdirection, or stubbornness, are used as a cover for incompetence. All of these behaviors get in the way of a successful migration. Double checking the validity of claims and issues raised during the migration can help uncover idiots. This is

> People rise to their level of incompetence – The Peter Principle

another reason to have the project run by someone who will not benefit politically.

None of the above:

These are a few of the random issues we have seen which bring a data migration to its knees. There will be more types of resistance to data migration. You have to decide whether an employee's reaction is natural and part of healthy skepticism, or if it's suspicious and unhealthy for your company.

> We presented a solution to a company, left our tools and software there to be implemented, and then were called back months later to have a meeting with the CEO. He ranted and raved and swore that it didn't work. We were shocked. Then the CEO said, "I actually invited you back to fire you as consultants." (We had been talking directly to the "workers bees" who were using our product over the course of those months, and they were saying it ran great for them.)
>
> I said, "Of course, if it's not saving you money then there is no fee, but may I ask a few questions for a post-mortem assessment?"

He said, "Sure."

I asked "Can we talk to the manager who installed our solution?"

He said, "That's reasonable."

The CEO used the phone in the conference room to call the IT department. The head of IT answered and said, "I don't know who installed it, but Sue, the manager over the data import team, told me the software didn't work. Can't you ask her?"

The CEO asked the receptionist to get Sue for him. She replied that Sue was at a doctor's appointment and was out the rest of the day. (Suspiciously enough, Sue had scheduled the meeting and we had talked to her that morning.)

The CEO tried to call Sue on her cell phone. She did not answer. The CEO was starting to get red in the face.

The CEO called the receptionist and asked her, "Is there anybody from Sue's team that is here?"

The receptionist put him on with George, the guy in the cubicle next to Sue.

The CEO asked a very nervous-sounding George, who had just told me the day before that the solution was beautiful, if he knew anything about the installation of our software and why it didn't work.

George said, "We never officially installed it. We were told to wait for confirmation that it worked. The demo is impressive. Can I officially install it now?"

The CEO said "Not right now, but thank you." Then he called a five-minute break.

It didn't matter if the company had never tried the software; we could hear him yelling at people from his office.

He came back, apologized, and said, "We'll actually install the software before we tell you it doesn't work. Oh, and if you speak to Sue before I do, tell her to call me."

Sue was fired (big surprise there), and the company eventually replaced the

CEO who couldn't get the solution, which was literally handed to him on a platter, installed.

However, the IT department sabotaged the product because their little empire would lose too many jobs, even though it worked in all the demonstrations, on their system, and with their data and people running the computer. They never could offer any explanation of why it didn't "work" when we were not in the room or what would go wrong with it.

The new CEO, in his first cost-cutting measure, canceled our contract, even though we never billed them a dime because it was never implemented.

Is your IT department part of the solution, or part of the problem? Do you know they are on board, or are they just playing for time?

Planning a Data Migration

If you don't know what you are building, you'll probably end up with something else. (Apologies for twisting Yogi Berra's quote)

There are many types of data migrations. We will concentrate on two types; everything going one-way to a new system, and integrating two or more systems. There are other types, but these are the most common. Everything written here will also apply to the other types of migrations.

Who should be in charge?

This key decision can make or break a migration effort. Depending on the corporate culture, the decision is often to choose a DBA, or a programmer to be in charge of a migration of the data. Have you ever heard the saying, "You can't see the forest for the trees"? DBAs and Programmers are usually the guys in the trench with no vision. You want someone up in a tree who says, "Hey! You're supposed to be going that way!" I recommend a Business Analyst, if you can find one. Consider hiring a consultant. Make sure from the beginning that everyone knows a bonus is riding on the success of the migration.

> Consider assigning a BA (Business Analyst) to perform the analysis of your company. Let him present his findings to you.

The most successful migrations I have been involved with have a Business Analyst (BA) in charge. The point of migrating data is to make your business run better, not to have a beautiful machine-code connection with the database. The point is not to let the programmer spend years writing elegant code, but to make the company more profitable and also make the users of the database and software happy.

If you do not have a BA (Business Analyst) in your company, this is a good time to get a consultant.

Warning! Shameless pitch ahead!

Buy them a copy of this book… ;-)

When you get down to the actual work of deciding what should go where, a BA will be invaluable as a member of the team.

A BA speaks English and "Geek." They can actually explain to you what you are doing in a language you'll understand, and not some technical jargon gibberish filled with buzzwords.

Lastly, using a BA will help if you suspect that a DBA or Programmer may try to turn the migration into job security by stretching it out for years. Does this mean a programmer or DBA can't run a conversion? No, but it does mean they have to understand that the business end of your company is the first priority. If you are lucky enough to have such an individual, promote them as far as they want to go, but no farther. Programmers and DBAs rarely want to be 100% management. They got into their profession for a reason, so don't promote them to a position where they won't be happy.

Migrating to a new system

When migrating to a new system, you need to have a "no-data-left-behind" mentality.

That means if there is a place to put the data from the old system, put it there, even if no one has a need for it now. Why? Because when someone wants that data later, the new data added since the migration could be a problem. What about a repeatable migration? That's GREAT! How do you plan to update a new field into an ongoing migration without having the possibility of overwriting something you didn't intend to? (It's a high-risk addition later, just do it right the first time.)

Migrating to a new system should be a repeatable process. The reason I call it a migration instead of conversion is that in a "perfect world" you will be able to use the old system and new system at the same time, and see the data in both. This may seem like extra work, but once you know where the data comes from, all you have to do is know how to run it in reverse. In this way, both the old and new systems stay in sync while each department is brought on-line one at a time. And with the right tools, that's simple. If your tools don't, or can't, do that, check out the tools on www.convertabase.com.

Migrating to a new system instead of just converting gives you several advantages:

- Pre-adoption testing of reports.

- Fewer overtime weekends for developers.

- High odds of the migration being considered successful.

- Gradual migration of users

    o Less impact on the bottom line

    o Less impact on support personnel

Migrating compared to Converting has only one drawback—it's more complex to set up, and thus a bit more time needs to be taken in the planning phases. In my experience, that time is easily recouped from the bugs that get exposed early on in the process that would have required handling later on the "Conversion".

Integrating two or more systems together

Two or more systems can be tied together. When you decide to migrate your data, you need to do it in a way that minimally impacts your business (the part that makes money).

Never plan to move to the new system and figure out the data later. That is how companies end up supporting two systems, with all the costs of two systems, for years!

In the ROI section you decided who and how. Now you need to decide when. Some of the reports and answers from the "How-to-know" section will prove very useful now; namely, the "Down Time" report.

Plan your conversion. Many data migrations are finished by someone other than the person who started them. Without a comprehensive, documented, clear, up-to-date plan, the assignment of a new project lead often means the work starts all over. With a good plan, the person taking over the project has a chance of completing it, documenting it, and being the hero for fixing what was heading toward a corporate disaster story.

Always plan to perform your development against a "Duplicate" or "Development" server. Once you have a snapshot of the data that you generate during "Down Time," you can develop against it without impacting your revenue-generating activities. I recommend going so far as to have the conversion and machines behind their own routers so the network traffic does not slow down corporate (money-making) processes. Periodically update your development server with data pulled during "Down Time".

Plan to implement your migration during "Down Time." Plan Tools and Milestones. At the milestones, plan for documentation to be updated. Plan for Testing, and plan for Reports.

You need to know how long the development will take. The time-frame is the most complicated piece to plan. I suggest that the person responsible for the project use a project management system; if you don't have MS Project™ you can get Open Workbench for free at: (http://www.openworkbench.org/). I recommend using a project management tool from the very beginning. Scheduling the planning meetings shows everyone this will be an organized project.

The details of the migration will vary by project, methodology, and tools, but no detail is too small to include in your project plan. Hardware that is not always accessible, vacation time, sick time, and weekends (I have been on a project where they forgot to schedule weekends; it was not a success. People tend to go home for the weekend anyway…)

> Don't show time allocated for risks to people on the project, or, they will plan to use it.

You may need to keep two charts, or better yet, two views of one chart. One will only include employee estimates. The other will show your estimates of risk as additional time. Don't show time allocated for risks to people on the project, because all tasks will then expand to fill the time allotted. If you don't have a formula for Risk Management, start with this:

Estimated Task Length * Risk Estimate * Risk impact = the amount of time that needs to be added to that step as risk mitigation (Estimates are in "Man Hours").

When you have a due date for the risk-included chart, that is what you plan for. Don't plan for the due date if nothing goes wrong. Again, don't publicize the risks- included date to your worker bees, but do use that date when talking to management. You can also show management the chart for worker bees.

How to make your plan successful:

1. The fact that you have a plan with actual timelines and milestones sets you miles ahead of most migration projects.

2. Get a nitpicker on the team. Everyone hates a nitpicker, but you want at least one person who won't "go along to get along" on your team. If you don't have one, consider hiring a consultant to be a nitpicker, consultants make great nitpickers especially when they know that's their job. (Buy them a copy of this book)

3. Make sure the person leading the team is not afraid to override the nitpicker when they need to. The nitpicker is there to raise flags, not halt the process completely. Overriding the nitpicker should be documented when it happens.

4. Tell whoever is in charge to follow the plan, even if things happen that were not planned for. Have him add a new step to the plan, revise, and inform management (you)

immediately of any shift in completion date. Tell him to trust you. You'd rather know bad news quickly so you can handle it, and not at the last minute when your options are gone.

5. Encourage your team to "conspire to succeed" with rewards for getting done ahead of the schedule. Have your team lead tell them all they were hand-picked for this project, offer project-based bonuses, consider giving them a half-day of vacation for every day the project is done early. You may want to delay the offer of rewards until the estimates for time are in though.

6. Be personally involved. Everyone on the team will feel like the project is more important if you attend the milestone meetings yourself, and even more so if you have read at least the summary on the documentation.

In summary, your plan should include:

- Put your project on a timeline.

- Include the Resources in the timeline.

- Make Contingency plans.

- Keep two timelines.

- Get a nitpicker on the team.

- Encourage them to conspire to succeed.

- Be involved.

Structuring a data migration

If you don't have a plan, how do you follow it and how do you know how close to "Done" you are?

There are three common methods of structuring a migration. They all have benefits and drawbacks. First I will list the structures, and then we will discuss the strengths and weaknesses of each. Know what method you are going to use before you get started; it will save you time.

- Direct migration

- Staging database

- Data Warehouse

Direct migration:

This is the easiest to understand. You import the data directly into the target database. While this is the fastest to run, and the fastest to start building, it has several drawbacks.

- Data has to be "Cleaned" in the target database, or the target database has to be "loose" enough to allow dirty data to be imported and cleaned there.

- Dirty Data may not insert into a strictly-structured database without errors.

- There is no easy way to back out of a failed conversion run. The development tends to be "Code, load, and explode."

- It provides for one-way transfer only. Two-way transfer becomes problematic.

Staging database:

For this method of Migrating data, the data is read from its source files or Database, and import it into an intermediate database designed to facilitate cleansing and validation before the import into the target database. This method provides the most flexibility and reliability, but that comes at a cost.

The drawbacks include:

- This intermediate database requires much more storage. This can be, and often is, on a separate machine from the target database; especially if space is a problem.

- This migration requires the data to be read and written twice at a minimum, so it takes longer.

- Staging your data requires a designed database for that purpose, so development takes longer.

The benefits include:

- This is the best option for cleansing really dirty (corrupted) data.

- This is a really good method if you have to bring data from more than one data source and correlate them before insertion into the Target database.

- If you are migrating data to a "Target" system from more than one system, building a staging database creates a reusable piece so the company saves time and money.

- If you want to validate totals, counts, or some other kind of validation requirement, it's much easier just to import validated data

- If you are importing from flat files (text), it can be a good way to create the data required by the target system from multiple files.

Data Warehouse:

A data warehouse is the biggest and best option for a large business. You design a database to hold all the information from all your systems and you bring all that data to this central location (metaphorically-speaking central). Then once you have all the data, you correlate it and clean it. All this data is then sent back out to all the different systems. So your shipping software has the same address as the sales department. Data warehousing is sometimes called the "one-view" strategy or a "single source of truth."

Most business analysis programs work best on a single data source. Data warehouses do have pluses and minuses too.

Let's look at the drawbacks:

- Data warehouses are always *under construction*.

- Data Warehouses require ongoing support personnel.

- Data Warehouses typically require an addition to hardware.

- Data Warehouses are complex and the development is costly.

- Data Warehouses still require data migrations with the target applications.

Benefits:

- Data Warehouses allows you to get reports on your whole business.

- Data Warehouses are required for real-time dashboards for some data.

- Data Warehouses provide a single source for backing up your data.

- Data warehouses facilitate some emergency relocation plans.

- Data Warehouses eliminate the need for complex conversions between multiple systems (like a wheel that has spokes, with the Data Warehouse at the middle as opposed to a spider's web with junctions scattered all over the place.)

- Data Warehouses can sometimes allow you to consolidate functions in your company into one system which were formerly separate systems.

As an administrator, you don't need to know the details, but it's good to understand what people are asking to build when these strategies are discussed.

Verifying a Data Migration

Avoid "Ready, Fire, Aim" or it will cost you.

You are probably saying, "Wait, don't we have to do it before we verify it?"

In short, no, you don't. You want to know what you are doing, and when you are done. This section helps you define that.

If you build the verification first, you have a target. If you don't have a target, you may not ever decide you are done. Build the verification first, and avoid scope creep. (Scope Creep is when your requirements keep changing, so the project never gets done)

Verification falls into several categories:

- Did all the records get moved? (Comparisons, record counts)

- Does everything add up to the same amount? (Accounts payable, receivable, inventory counts, etc., done by comparisons and sums)

- Add validations as appropriate. Most of this can be placed into a report that runs automatically at the end of the migration as an automated way to know how well the conversion is going as you are building it.

- Automatically build a report on the success or failure you are having with every run. (For meeting milestones!)

Check the reports that come with a new platform, or software. Reports can vary by different versions of the same piece of software. When the canned reports are vastly different, it's less of a problem. Similar-looking reports can lead people to think they are "identical" when they are not:

> I was on the team for a migration to a new version of software.
>
> We spent two weeks on "crash overtime" trying to find a million dollars that had disappeared from a report the CEO relied on.
>
> Finally, the money was discovered! It was on page three. No one told him the new report had moved a line item from page one to page three.
>
> This kind of report "misunderstanding" is more commonly an emergency when you do a one-time "Conversion" instead of a data migration where the CEO and others have a chance to run their reports long before the "drop dead" date.

> If the CEO in this story had seen the reports in advance, telling him the item was on page three would have been easy. Instead, when the company had made the jump, and there was no way back, he focused so tightly on the bottom line that no one wanted to be the one to say, "Are you reading the report right?"

Always build your validation set, and get sign off before starting the conversion or you will never know when you have succeeded.

> I worked with a large multinational corporation, and as their projects would slip, they would have meetings where they would redefine the meaning of "success" on a regular basis to protect everyone's bonuses. Moving the targets closer is not my definition of "Success."

If you want the migration done correctly and on time, give your team a clear target; Define "success" first, and firmly.

Build your verification first, and then build your migration to pass the tests everyone has agreed define success.

Enjoy your reputation as a genius…

Executing a data migration

How to build and test:

Have your methodology, documentation requirements, tests, and verification all defined. How you do it is simple: you follow the plan.

There are three basic ways to actually "Execute" a data migration:

- Code, Load, and Explode. (CLE or one-off code)

- Hire it done by a consultant, or corporation.

- Do it with your personnel, but use tools.

CLE

This is the most common, and least successful, method of performing a migration. The thought is usually, "We have programmers, why don't they work on this project too?"

Consider these points:

- You have programmers because there is a job for them to do. Ask them what is on their plate already. Is the migration important enough to put all their current work on hold?

- Are any of your programmers skilled in data conversion?

- Will they need training?

- What is the risk to the success of this project by writing one-off code?

I call this "Code, Load, and Explode" for a reason. The programmer usually ends up writing a piece of code, running it, and watching it blow up. Then he tries to find the place in the code where the error happened. It may be his code, or something in the data that only happens once. Since CLE is seldom modular, the Migration will have to be run over and over to debug it. Error handling must be added when errors happen. I have seen (because I was assigned to work on them) CLE's that would run for hours before the error would happen. Days and weeks can be eaten up just tracking down a single bug.

I'd like to say a word about tools, and encouraging your people to write tools:

> I was on a project once that required triggers to be built for 200 tables. Each trigger was dependent on the structure of the table, so any change meant rebuilding them. The team members who were in charge of the database were projecting later and later completion dates, as changes were made to both the trigger's output and

the tables. (At this point, the programmers were projecting that they would complete about a month after the product shipped.) I was on another part of the project and ahead of schedule.

The manager over the project assigned me to help them "get back on track".

I was less than welcome. They didn't want some fancy-pants know-it-all to show them up. They had been building all the triggers by hand.

I asked for a backup of the current database, and they refused. Then I asked for access to it, so I could "try a few things"… I got my backup copy.

I went back to my desk and created a Trigger-writing program. The next day, I went to their area and asked them to back up their database. They were reluctant, but I threatened to run my test on their live, un-backed up database—and they backed it up.

I ran my program. With a single button click, I dropped all the triggers they had created so far. (This was not a popular move)

Then I selected all the tables they were supposed to build Triggers for from a list of tables in my program, and generated the triggers with another click.

Poof! They were now "caught up".

I showed them how my tool worked and handed the DBA (DataBase Administrator) a CD with the source.

I asked them, "So, do you guys need me anymore?" They were glad to tell me no.

At the meeting later that day, the database team reported that they had caught up. The manager looked at me and said, "What happened?" (The database team glared at me)

I said, "*They* had a brilliant idea, and they didn't need me after all."

My manager looked suspicious, but let it go for the time being. The database team looked shocked that I had not taken credit so they would look bad.

Later the Manager pulled me aside and said, "You had the idea, didn't you?"

I responded, "Prove it. Besides, do you really want them to resent my help when they need it next?"

He said, "No, never mind."

Weeks later, when he was assigned a tough assignment, the DBA came over and asked for some advice on building tools. Success! And the DB team didn't end up hating me after all. Success times two!

Encourage your employees to build tools as solutions in their coding. It will improve the tools they write for you, too. (Do a Google lookup for "dogfooding")

Consultant or Consulting Corporation (I'll just use consultant from here):

Consultants are a mixed bag. Some consultants are a great option, and some consultants have no idea what they are doing. The trick is telling the difference. Things to look for:

- Buzz words; if they only speak in jargon, they probably only know jargon.

- Free suggestions. You want the kind of people who want you to succeed, even if you don't hire them.

- Have your DBA talk to the guy who will be doing the work (The DBA should interview him.) If you don't have a DBA, then have your most technical or knowledgeable person about the current system do the interview.

- Often, a DBA or techie can tell in just a few minutes if the consultant has done this before, and if he knows what he is talking about.

- The DBA will be working closely with this person. Letting him have input makes the process more likely to succeed.

- Have the consultant tell you who he has done this for previously. (You don't want someone who hasn't ever done this before)

- Does the consultant have references you can check?

Only engage a consultant if:

- They agree to build the target first, and then shoot for that target. (Building the target around the arrow is failure.)

- They accept your definition of a target (Suggestions are great, but your company should ultimately make the decision).

- They understand and agree that you need documentation at every milestone (or more often).

- They agree that you own the process.

Things to consider:

- If they have a team, you might hire your own consultant to be part of their team and report directly to you on progress.

- Consultants often work on an hourly rate, so speed is not in their best interest.

- Change orders can kill your budget. Encourage your employees to decide up front what they want, and stick to it. You may even consider requiring departments that make changes to pay the change fee from their own department. Decide and explain your method to your people before you start.

- If a consultant is going to use a tool, does that tool build documentation?

- Are there per-machine fees, server licenses, or other fees that you will have to pay to use their tools or service?

- Can you get access to any tools they used after they're is gone? (What will that cost?)

- Is there support? (Especially important if this is going to be an on-going process.)

Do it yourself with Tools:

Doing it yourself with tools can be an attractive option, if you have the personnel. This is especially important if your people will have to maintain the system after a permanent migration is up and running. If you are going to eliminate personnel from support of the old system, consider retraining them to perform the migration. When looking at tools, consider the following:

- How much does training cost? Is it on-site, off-site, web-based, or in a book?

- How much does a license cost? Is it per record, per machine, or one fee to the company, and is there a designer fee, a service, or some other delivery method?

- Will you need a new license every year, every month?

- Are there support options?

- Does this tool produce documentation?

- How flexible is this tool? What if we need to do something in a piece of our own code? Will they let us do that?

- Can I add my own comments to the steps, code, or whatever they are using to configure their tool?

- Is there a way to print out the comments and notes?

- Can you try before you buy?

The Tools on http://www.convertabase.com:

- Have free online training, and on-site Training is available.

- Licenses are available for 10¢ a record, or when you reach 25,000 records, you buy an unlimited number for $2,500 a month.

- A new license is needed every month for the unlimited on-line tools, but 500 records are free every month.

- If Convertabase performs your conversion for you, they will support it. Support is available for the tools.

- Convertabase's tools automatically generate documentation as an external HTML file direct from the source.

- Convertabase supports calls to external programs as part of their process.

- Convertabase's tools will automatically generate some notes, allowing the person generating the migration to add or replace whatever they want in those notes.

- Convertabase allows the developer to produce documentation for only the objects selected by the developer.

- Convertabase offers a free trial of their designer online.

If you can't find out this kind of information about a tool, how do you know it's the right tool?

Documenting your data migration

This is often the most neglected, and ridiculed, step of a data migration. Once it is complete, you need to document what you have done. Why? It may be a while, but the odds are that someone, someday, will need to look at the code, Script, or configuration file again. The odds are also good that the developer who set up the migration will not be the person who needs to look at the code.

> I worked for a large company at one point as a contractor; they had a migration that had been running for three years.
>
> Due to HIPAA regulations, they were required to make a change to the import that was reading in Records written by a mainframe.
>
> Since I was already there setting up another Migration, they handed this to me over my objections. It was one-off code, and I was told the Source was on the server….
>
> I searched all the source code servers I had access to.
>
> I found only two out of seven files, which by themselves were completely unusable.

Management had the original programmer flown in. He still worked for the company, but was now in another state.

I went into the meeting to explain to him what I had found, and he exploded. "You lost the source code?!"

The Manager explained that they had temporarily transferred him back, and hopefully, with the two of us working together, we could still make the deadline which was three weeks away.

The Programmer said to us, "You can't make me go through another three months of hell! I quit!" He laid his name badge on the table and stalked out of the room.

As you can imagine, there was a moment of stunned silence, and one of the managers turned to me and said, "Um, help?"

I told them, "Forget one-off code. We'll never be done in time. Can I please use my tools now?"

They said, "On one condition. Once you meet the deadline, you then write some code to do the same thing. It's company standard. Anything we maintain has to be in code, so your one-time migration can use your tools, but the code you write will hopefully run until we are no longer over IT."

The migration was importing approximately seven million records from a complex. The definition had a "Having Clause" which makes it variable length. It was a COBOL record, and ran for three days. My new import, running on the same hardware, and using the same database back-end, ran in three hours. When it was re-written into code that was not as optimized as the Convertabase tools suite, it ran in seven hours.

Why is this in the documentation section?

Because one of the features of this migration tool was a point-and-click builder for documentation. Using the wizards in the tools, I quickly replicated the migration using that documentation. In a week, total, I had their solution. Then I had to start writing code to duplicate what the tools were doing. Sigh.

Documentation can make or break a future alteration to a migration. It can also answer difficult or awkward questions like, "What did this do for us?" It can explain when people want to know why something was, or was not, migrated. Look for tools that automatically write documents, and documents that contain notes written by the developer.

Planning for the future

There are very few rules with no exceptions, and this is one of them. Someday, someone will want data pulled from your new system, or will want to integrate with your new system. How hard is it going to be to do that?

Things to consider:

- What is the life expectancy of your system? (You should know that for ROI calculations anyway)

- What is your growth rate in the current system? (You should be able to get a report about that)

- Can you archive old data to decrease your growth rate? (If you can, is it in the plan?)

- Can you expand the maximum capacity of your system? (If you can, is it in the plan?)

- Is there documentation that could help people in the future? (If not, why not?)

- Can you decrease the growth rate without decreasing profits? (How much would that cost? Calculate the ROI)

Start planning for the next upgrade as soon as this one is complete.

- Can your new system provide reports that it is not currently providing that would be useful?

- Can we build a dashboard that will give us better access to live data?

- Can we now automate stuff that was manual with the old system?

- Laying these things out in a document allows you to review it every six months and can delay your next migration expense.

Business process system

As a leader in your business, you know that the money-making which happens is a process. You change that process only when you think there is a better way to make money. Some business processes are patented, some are trade secrets, and some are even franchised.

Let's look at some well-known franchise business processes. McDonalds® has a process that tells its franchisees how much to charge, how to prepare the product, and even how long the product can sit before it is disposed of. McDonalds® has similarities and differences from Wendy's. The similarities in the business they're in create some similarities in their process. The variations in their processes determine the differences in their profitability. I'm not going to argue which one has better "food," but I think everyone will agree they have different profitability.

Your business process produces a product, and the product is what you sell to make money. The Process is overhead expense. The more of the expenses in your overhead you can eliminate, the more profitable you are.

Some questions you should ask yourself and your employees are:

- How well do you know your process?

- Could you know it better?

- Ask your employees what they think their job description is.

- Compare what your employees think their job description is with what you have in HR for them.

The odds are that you will find things you didn't know were part of your process.

I know the owner of the company with this problem:

There was a very large company that had a process they wanted automated, but no one could tell us the entire process.

This particular process involved the routing of a document.

A document was submitted to this process printed on red paper so it could be tracked easier. People took turns following it through the "process." They had to watch it 24/7, because some things were done by several shifts of employees.

This document went through iterative transfers that had the same document hit the same inbox several times. The document would collect stamps and notations that it had been seen by others, since it was there.

Finally, after two weeks, the document was placed in a file cabinet. The people involved in the process were interviewed.

Most of these people had inherited their part of the process from their predecessor with no explanation. To quote one person, "When I got the job that is what my trainer did with these documents, so that's what I do. I have no idea why."

When the "process" was shown to management, they were incredulous, but agreed that this two-week process could be replaced with an automated system, which would eliminate several jobs, and free up time on many others.

Even if you are not going to automate the whole process, knowing your business process can save your company money, and provide transparency for what can be a convoluted process.

Workflow Process Systems (WPS)

> Make everything as simple as possible, but no simpler.
> - Albert Einstein

A WPS helps corporations reduce costs by increasing efficiency or reducing personnel. Steps in the WPS often replace processes that used to be manual. A WPS is characterized by a special table in one or more databases to track the progress of units of work.

Let's describe a simple WPS:

Col	Column Name	Type
1	Index	Number
2	Order	Text
3	Status	Number
4	Last_Access	Time

This table is a simple WPS table. Some are simpler, and some are more complex. Some have a table to track history, error state, etc.

This is an example of a simple workflow process.

Let's describe a simple business process:

Step	Description
1	Received order
2	Order in Process
3	Order Shipping
4	Order Error
5	Order Completed

You receive an order. You process the order. You ship the order. If anything bad happens, you set the order to "error" and look at it later. Automating this process will show the usefulness of the workflow process system.

- A new order is entered into the system from a web site.

- If the entry program doesn't put things in the database, tools can.

- When the order is processed, a person or program marks it ready to ship.

- When the order has shipped, it is marked completed.

- If you want a "Dashboard" for your WPS, you can often track (1) latency (2) counts over periods of time and (3) count for each process.

If you track averages by day, for example, you can see if a step is getting faster or slower. You can add resources to your slowest step and remove them from your fastest one to streamline the whole process. If your business process involves something that can be automated, you can now see where to optimize with additional machines.

How do tools like Convertabase's fit into this?

Convertabase can perform any of the functions required to automate, or even create, a WPS. Convertabase can help with design or execution. Convertabase's Packages can create a whole process, or "Wrapper" processes that need to be a part of the WPS.

Case Study:

> If you are adding a new step to a WPS and Bob, who has been doing this step, is retiring, this is what you should do:
>
> Bob's job was looking at the "next" document listed in the database and reformatting all the dates from one format to another. (I have changed Bob's name, but I have seen this step in a WPS)

Convertabase can add legacy steps to your WPS.

Bob was manually setting the process flag for the next process.

Your company creates a package or program that checks for documents to process, reformats the date(s) in the document, and sets the correct flag. We label this process the "Bob Replacement" process.

Bob monitors the process for his last few weeks, and retires secure in the knowledge that the WPS will continue to process documents successfully without him.

The company replaces an employee (expensive) with a computer (cheap) that runs 24/7.

If more documents come in than a single computer can keep up with, the package / program is simply copied to a second computer (or as many extra computers as are needed) and your process is "scaled up".

If your WPS is really small, all processes may run on one computer.

WPS are a good idea for all companies because the more you automate, the less you have to do yourself.

If you don't have a WPS in your business, consider the ROI. Do that math and find out if there is a migration you might want to do as well.

Epilog:

In this book we covered a lot of ground. ROI, Data Migration, Overcoming Resistance, Employee Questionnaires, Documentation, and even making your business more efficient with a WPS. Through it all, we have had the focus of making your company more profitable, and helping you to find more "Pay-at-the-Pump" solutions. This is a perspective that is profit-center driven. We hope that by sharing this book, even with those not needing a data conversion, we've helped make your company make more money.

Thank you for reading our book.

Jerry Hayward
Sam Shumway